No More

MS

Depression

MS-101

Ramon Hyron Garcia

BALBOA.
PRESS

A DIVISION OF HAY HOUSE

Balboa Press books may be ordered through booksellers or by contacting:

Balboa Press
A Division of Hay House
1663 Liberty Drive
Bloomington, IN 47403
www.balboapress.com
1 (877) 407-4847

Printed in the United States of America.

ISBN: 978-1-4525-8449-2 (sc)
ISBN: 978-1-4525-8450-8 (e)

Balboa Press rev. date: 12/19/2013

We are in the middle of a chronic disease pandemic. In the United States more people die from chronic disease than any other cause. What most people don't know is that chronic disease is preventable. When it is already present it's course can be altered. Not by a pill or a surgery but by personal choice.

Chronic disease results from chronic inflammation. This is best understood as the body being on fire. Fires are dealt with by deprivation of fuel and oxygen. Unhealthy food is the fuel and negative thoughts and emotions are the oxygen that allow the fire of chronic inflammation to rage in the body. The right foods can act like a fire retardant. Positive thoughts have the ability to alter the bodies physiology and making it less susceptible to an inflamed state.

This story is about a man's journey with a chronic disease called Multiple Sclerosis. A neurologic disease that results from the breakdown of cells in the brain and spinal cord. It is a chronic and debilitating condition that modern medicine has struggled to deal with. Ray found relief from the realization of the importance of input. What he put into himself made a difference. Be it positive emotions or ingesting an abundance of vegetables these "inputs" reduce inflammation. Multiple Sclerosis has been described as the brain on fire. Ray has found with himself just as I have found with my patients that what you put in determines what you get out. We truly are what we eat.

It is a liberating story about choice. Ray shares his choices in a personal manner. This will resonate with many and inspire others to make the choice to eliminate the chronic inflammation in their lives.

Michael A. Arata, MD

 **Synergy Health Concepts**
4501 Birch St. Newport Beach, CA 92660
Call us toll free at 877-792-2784 or 949-221-0129

Medical Disclaimer

(1) No advice
      This Book contains general information about medical conditions and treatments. The information is not advice and should not be treated as such.

(2) Credit
      This document was created using a Legal template.

(3) No warranties
      The medical information in this book is provided without any representations or warranties express or implied. We make no representations or warranties in relation to the medical information in this book.

      Without prejudice to the generality of the foregoing paragraph, we do not warrant or represent that the medical information in this book:
      (a) Will be constantly available, or available at all; or
      (b) is complete, true, accurate, up to date or non-misleading.

(4) Professional assistance
      You must not rely on the information in this book as an alternative to medical advice from your doctor or other professional healthcare provider.

      If you have any specific questions about any medical matter, you should consult your doctor or other professional healthcare provider.

      If you think you may be suffering from a medical condition, you should seek immediate medical attention.

Forword

Study after study has shown that the environment, that is diet, exercise level and smoking accounted for 70 to 95% of the risk for acquiring diabetes, heart disease, obesity, cancer and autoimmune problems. Yet the vast majority of the physicians use medication and surgical procedures to treat their patients instead of teaching them how lifestyle impacts health. The doctors who treat multiple sclerosis are no different. The vast majority of MS specialists are no different. They rely only on medication and know nothing about the impact of diet and lifestyle on MS disease progression and severity.

Like Ramon, I have multiple sclerosis and was severely disabled by my disease. In 2007, I could walk short distances with two walking sticks. It was hard to sit up. I was having more brain fog. I am a physician, and I had been studying the medical research using pubmed.gov, to see if I could find something that might slow my disease progression. That summer, based upon my review of the scientific research, Paleo principles and Functional Medicine, I created a protocol that lead to a dramatic improvement in function. One year later I was able to walk throughout the hospital without a cane, and even complete an 18 mile bicycle ride with my family.

I was like Paul on the way to Damascus. The old me had been struck down, replaced by someone who understood that diet and lifestyle are far more powerful at creating health and treating disease than medication. How I practiced medicine changed; instead of relying on prescriptions I spent time teaching people why and how to eat and live for health. I shifted my research from diagnostic error to nutrition and lifestyle as treatment for progressive MS. I also teach the public and the health professionals about the utility of diet and lifestyle to treat chronic disease.

In this book, Ramon Garcia, shares his journey with MS. He too was severely disabled due to MS and was wheelchair bound. But since addressing diet and lifestyle he has dramatically improved his function, health and vitality. He is not alone. More people are discovering that diet and lifestyle do have a dramatic impact on whether our disease will progress or regress. Whatever health challenge that you are experiencing, you can begin to shift your diet and lifestyle choices to health promoting ones. You can begin to improve your health with your choices, just as Ramon did.

Terry Wahls, MD
Author, The Wahls Protocol How I Beat Progressive MS Using Paleo Principles and Functional Medicine

www.wahlsprotocol.com

Why I wrote this book

This book was inspired by a number of people, looking around I see too many people giving up, this is just not acceptable to me. So when I had to deal with my own demons, i.e.: when I fell sick with my last relapse I wanted to give up. I found new ways by researching physical therapy, to heal myself and I read the Bible, knowing to not give up and to not speak negativity into existence. So I wrote this book as a beginner's guide to show there is hope. Just have faith in God and yourself and know that you are stronger than what you believe. There are others out there who want you to be weaker than you believe, so this book is to show how I became stronger than what others thought and to accomplish what they said I would not be able to do. Now I hope you learn a lot from this book and you start doing your own research. This is just an outline that you will use towards your goal and fill in the blanks to win your own battles. Never give up and never let someone tell you what you can or cannot do. Make up your own mind as to what you can or cannot do.

This is why I wrote this book, to give hope, to give help and to give strength to the weak. You can and you will look everyday in the mirror and say "I can, I will and I'm strong,

I will never give up and I will get through this". Know that you are what you say you are and do not accept the things in life you do not want. In my opinion, accepting is a sign that you give up.

Table of Contents

Introduction

First, I am not a medical professional. These are my stories, my theories and my opinions. Please seek additional medical help if needed. This is just my story of how I dealt with MS in my life. I just want to share my story and to give hope to the hopeless.

HI, my name is Ramon Hyron Garcia. I'm a 36 year old (at the time of writing this book) divorced father of 1 boy, Christian Rey Taijeron Garcia. I was adopted at 2 days old by an African American family and was raised as a pastor's kid in a loving, large family.

I also deal with RRMS <relapsing remitting multiple sclerosis> and was diagnosed in 2003 at Loma Linda Medical Center in beautiful southern California.

This is my story of how I took grim news 7 years after my diagnosis and made it work in my favor! I hope and pray you all can take from my weakness and strength to forge your own armor to fight through the depression and negative thoughts that this HORRIBLE disease brings!

I also want to share how I went from 275+ lbs to 202 lbs in 7 months or less and from NOT being able to do 10 pushups to being able to do 120+ a day. Feeling the loneliness that NO ONE understands and going on to helping others cope with the same issues; my mail box and phone does NOT stop with positive messages' . . . .

Sunday Morning, (December 2009) like the 4 others before it, I walked out my front door on the way to church. ALL of a sudden I fell backwards to the ground and could NOT move. I had to lie on the ground 3 hours before my next door neighbor finally helped me back in the house. A short time later he also took me to the ER where they just wrote me off as having Bells Palsy. OK, I had denied MS since 2003 and it is now December 2009. So, not taking care of myself, smoking, a horrible diet, and STRESS did a number on me. I was struck down.

Three months later I was sent home from the ER with medicine to treat Bells Palsy NOT MS. I was steadily getting worse. I became so weak I could not sit up without help and I lost vision in my left eye. After 2 months of ER trips I just gave up!

March 1st 2010 I wanted to get out of my bed; remember 2+ months earlier I needed help to even move and I tried to go to the rest room. I fell out of my bed and my cell phone was still on my bed. I tried for the next 4 to 5 hours to do everything I could to get to it.

As a lot of you know when you use energy in MS you DO NOT GET IT BACK right away. Once I finally reached my phone I dialed 911. THEN it took me 2 hours to arm crawl across the floor to the door to let in the EMT's. All this time I was on my cell phone BEGGING the 911 dispatcher NOT to let the EMT's break my door in!

NOW in the emergency room they, of course, ran every test in the book. I swear I was a pin cushion. The Doctor ordered an MRI for the next morning. I still denied I dealt with MS and they had NO clue to even look for it. After a night of incontinence and blood draws, being asked to wake up every 2 hrs for blood pressure and NEW pills to take there were still no clues. By the time 8 am rolled around I was off to take the MRI. After 1 ½ hours of being in that coffin (the MRI machine) they confirmed MS almost immediately. I had 27 brain lesions. This was consistent with my diagnosis in 2003 where an MRI scan showed 26 lesions. By the way, a little over a year ago (2012) my last MRI only showed 15 lesions!

So now I'm in my hospital bed, unable to move, blind in 1 eye and cannot use my voice. The Neurologist ordered rehab to see if I could regain my old self. I'll tell you now; being trapped in your own thoughts is the scariest movie you can ever imagine and the worst nightmare you'll ever have.

OK, now I am transferred to the rehab floor. I had probably 6 doctors come in and tell me I have to see this other doctor and do these other tests . . . . I did not know any better, NOR did I have any family there to help.

So starts my new life after 30 yrs of being "normal". I have to relearn to walk, relearn minor motor skills, relearn to talk, even things like dressing myself to brushing my teeth, to even relearning how to use the restroom . . . . Bathing me was so complicated, it came much later.

Had to visit a mock apartment to see if it was safe for me to transfer to the toilet, to the tub, to the sink WHILE in a wheel chair . . .

In Rehab care, I was made to keep a journal on EVERYTHING, i.e.: my goals, how to become what I was, how to regain a normal life. I honestly believe there is almost MORE stress being there and trying to get help.

Well, 8 months pass and I can now WALK with a walker for a short period of time, but mostly my life at the time is in a wheel chair. For some reason unknown to me I was told I was being transferred to a hospice . . .

The hospice. I had no idea what this was . . . . They told me it was a "nursing care facility to continue my rehab" ya right! I was the youngest person ever to go there, even the nurses were over 42 years if age, the next youngest patient was 63 years of age and I was 31 . . . .

AT this point I told myself I was NOT going to stop.

This brings me to the motivation and instruction contained in this book, MS101 and then the advanced lessons that I will be illustrating in the subsequent books.

CHAPTER 1

Your Doctor & Getting Started

It's a very lonely feeling when you hear that you're dealing with MS. In this chapter I will outline some things that I did when I was diagnosed and how I've dealt with it over the years. The first thought is unbelief, the second is fear, the third is "why me"? Now we all of deal with this scenario and this is what I've done; just try to smile and understand that is not the end it is not over. I know it's really hard but flex your muscles and say "is this all you got"? I'll tell you right now you're stronger than what THEY say you are. What you need to do is start to look for groups and information about what you are about to go through. This is no easy task but I hope this book will show you small steps to start towards a life filled with joy, happiness and no stress. What I did was first open the Internet and search for what treatments were available. I wish I knew about the diet stuff earlier. If you look deeper into what causes MS, you'll see that 99% of everything you're afflicted with heals with food! Do not get discouraged, there is hope. There are people out there who want to help and who want to talk. Always listen to what someone has to say, even if it doesn't seem like it pertains to you now because you never know what can come in handy.

The second thing I've done was look to see what support groups are in my area, just to see what others say nonnegative about MS. Do not listen to the negativity surrounding MS. But listen to any advice you get, and use it to help yourself if it's positive.

You will not look like you once did, you may not talk as well as you once did and you may have pain, numbness and tingling, you may be depressed and you may have incontinence, you may fall down and a host of other things might happen. They will say you'll need someone to help you with your life. This is simply not true. My life is living proof of that. But you need a good attitude or like I say P.M.A. Positive Mental Attitude. A good diet and exercise with the drive and determination to not give up! In this book you will read opinions of what I've done to get to the point where I can walk 6 miles in 100° weather. I moved across the country by myself, no Dr. cleared me to walk, to talk or to move cross country. I was never released from needing a wheelchair, but I walk without assistance. I take a cane to steady myself when I go for a walk. I have done this all on my own, with a good attitude and good diet and the drive to never ever give up!

One of the things not to do is bundle it all up and not talk to anybody. Let it go, put your pride behind you and remember you're dealing with something others may not be able to deal with. This is nothing to be embarrassed about, hold your head high, and show MS you won't take this lying down. You are stronger than this; do not let others dictate how your life is going to be and how it's going to end. Tomorrow is not promised; therefore don't live with the thought that yours will end tomorrow. But also live life with purpose, eat healthy, be healthy, just get up and do things. Even on days when you don't want to do anything try to do something, take control of your body and don't let MS tell you what your body can do for you. It's a key in positive motivation for you. If you're unable to motivate yourself no one else can motivate you, you need to find the drive and it is something you can do. That's what you do with MS. That's what I've done with MS. And I've always been the one to do things for others not myself, so I know what it's like to not want to do things for me. If you need more motivation than this look to your children, look to your wife, your husband, mom, dad, or anybody that you care for, it could be a best friend, it even could be a pet, just find the motivation. You know where to find it, only you can take control of your life. So don't let a man/woman/doctor tell you what you should do with your life!

CHAPTER 2

Attitude

You have to acquire something that I consider the biggest, most important thing you need to have; Positivity in MS. Figure out a way or find a way in your life to stay happy, stay motivated and to see the positive. Do not be negative. Is stress one of your worst enemies with MS? Then stress is a killer no matter what you're doing. But what I tend to do is to find the funny. Like tripping over the air, I act like everybody's watching and laughing. If I laugh first it is nothing if someone else laughs. We all take the good with the bad and the fact of the matter is we deal with this mess, so find the way to laugh because you will awaken tomorrow to deal with MS. MS is going to be there with you whether you like it or not. So make the best of the situation that you are not able to get out of at this particular time. Fight with a smile on your face. I tend to resort to this ideology that what I can deal with, I will . . . and I let God take care the rest. It is going to boil down to a choice. Like they say in the movie Shawshank Redemption, "Either get busy living, or get busy dying"! I also say "being negative is like rocking in a rocking chair, you're moving but you don't go anywhere". I seem to choose to live, to smile, to be happy! But ultimately the choice yours. Either beat this or not. I hope you choose to beat this!

Keep a good attitude no matter what you do. I was taught a long time ago by a friend younger than myself to either just deal with the problem and then get mad . . . or get mad when you subdue the problem. I find it better just to deal with the problem and then deal with my emotions later on. But to each their own.

But because I say find the funny, I always find a reason to smile and so I try to make fun of myself. Make sure you smile, laugh, just have a good time. Most important is just to be good to yourself. Be good to the person next to you, this will all bless you in the end. Make the MS an emotion not a disease and make it something that you can just get rid of. It's your choice, not the choice someone else who sits in an office in a white coat, although they are very important they're not the end-all in saying what your health is and will be. They have years and years of knowledge and training, but remember it's their advice to you, advice not fact. You change how your body is and how it responds to any sickness or negative effect! It's a Soul/Mind/Body connection. Mostly to be that person, who when their feet hit the floor, MS says "oh no"! Smile; show yourself and everyone else that nothing can get you down. Smile not only for yourself but everyone around you. Be happy and positive in everything you do. Know that you are winning and you will win. So with all this if you change your outlook, you change your outcome!

Another reason smile, you never know who is watching. Your story affects all others around you. Be happy and proud of what you had to go through to deal with in MS. Your attitude will also show your emotional state, if you have a positive emotional state things will seem better, therefore your whole outlook will be better to deal with MS, or diabetes, or even high blood pressure. Later in this book you will get an extensive lesson in diet. It is a great chapter written by my own close personal friend Jacqueline Joy.

She has a lot of knowledge in the area of diet and spent the last 4 to 5 years perfecting her diet. I stand to learn from her, I hope you will learn great things through her writing and knowledge. But like all things it's a piece to the MS puzzle. Everything you read about in this book is just one piece after another after another to our puzzle, but the ultimate cure is you, your attitude, your emotion, your drive and your determination to win. So never give up, always go on to something with the attitude that you will win, that you will succeed. Remember you don't fail, you just learn how not to do something next time.

CHAPTER 3

Do Not Get Frustrated

The important thing is not to get frustrated by what you are doing with MS. Just stay focused on how you deal with it and not look at the bad things that come along. Look at all the good. A lot of people don't tend to focus on the positive side of what's happening. Say for instance, someone could take one step and they are mad because they did not take 30. See, if you take one step it is better than zero steps. This would be a win. Don't get frustrated, just take two tomorrow. Just because it is hard to walk today it does not mean you're not going to walk 2 miles tomorrow, so don't get down. Think big, really big. And stay positive. Work at walking 2 miles tomorrow. Do what you can and smile after you do it, knowing that MS does not want you to be able to do anything. Frustration is the thing that tries to stop you from seeing what you can do. Do not let fear stop you from doing what you're able to do right now. Know that fear is here just to stop you. That is a product of frustration. If you get frustrated and you slow down, want to stop, just don't know that you can do more, frustration, fear, and mild pain want you to give up. But we are MS warriors we don't give up! When you get to the point of frustration, know that you are more than that, try to do 5%-10% more. Always know you can do more than what you think. Believe you can do more than what you think, see it in everything you do. Be determined. This should help get rid of frustration. Know that there will be frustrating times and there will be bad times, just rest, get up and do it again. The point is don't stop, keep going, keep your head up and keeps moving forward.

MS has a lot of tools in its arsenal to stop you and frustration is the biggest one. Frustration is one of those emotions you control, you get to control it, and it is yours. So you are going to decide if you're frustrated or not, if you give up or not, but as long as you know that it happens, it helps you be prepared for when it happens. So this is just one tool that you'll need to fight and beat MS. I hope all that you've read so far have been weapons to help you fight, and help you build a strong bridge over MS. Remember you can do it, you will win!

Chapter 4

Gauging Progress

In this chapter I want to tell you guys about gauging your progress. Do not get down if you have a setback. For example, if you fall, that is one small misstep compared to the 30, 40 or 50 steps you've taken in the past few days and probably a lot more. Many of us deal with things that are very embarrassing. This is why I say in my second chapter to make sure you surround yourself with people who are a positive influence. Because then you're not going to gauge the progress of the negativity but gauge the progress of the positivity. This is going to help you smile and see the smaller improvements that become big improvements. Honestly, if you look at it, you have small decreases that you think are big decreases. In a positive mind you will tend to look at the positive and not look at the negative. So remember never look at the shoulda/woulda/coulda's and focus on the shoulds/woulds/can-do's. A helpful habit to develop is to take the "t" off can't, won't and wouldn't and turn it into can, will and should. Remember a half of a step is better than no steps at all because you are half step further than you were before. I don't know about you but that is a progress not a negative. These are the things you should be looking at, not focusing on what you have not done, but focus on what you are able to do.

I say all the time, dream what you want to happen, go where you want to go and don't allow anyone or anything, like MS, diabetes or the thought of negativity like being over/under weight or someone else's perception stop you from being the best you that you can be. No one is like you. So do not let someone else's opinion change who you are. Most people have no clue how or what to think they would do if they dealt with MS or diabetes, or anything major in their life. It would be looked at as a negative. This why, in my opinion, people hide what they are embarrassed about. The thought of someone else's opinion about you is so powerful people have to hide. I do understand there are people out there who just want to hurt you and I know there are things out there like MS and other things that are there to hurt you. So embrace it, smile, laugh, and say that's what you deal with.

So with all this being said, look to the positive in your progress not the negative. This should help you see a better way to gauge your progress. Fighting this battle is a series of small wins. If you always look for the big wins you might miss the little ones and always see the negativity. Remember you can and you will win!

Chapter 5

Getting Support

In this chapter we will talk about making sure you have support. YOU are your biggest critic. Someone who's there to help you by showing you things that could help you walk better, speak better, eat better, or just all around do things better and improve your being overall. Make sure you take constructive criticism with a smile for any advice is better than no advice. You don't have to accept what everyone says, but listen because you never know when that bit of advice will come in handy. Everyone's experience is different than yours. No two people are the same, therefore no two express themselves the same and also the fact is no two MS conditions are the same! Remember even though we don't claim to have anything negative in our life, we don't ignore the negative things that tried to hurt us. This is why I say you must stay positive. Find the good, find the funny. Always have a smile for no one can walk your road the way you do.

Surround yourself with people who will boost you up, keep you happy and make good suggestions. Not the ones who will put roadblocks and obstructions in your way. We all know who those people are, so distance yourself from negative influence. I know it's easier said than done, but also remember if it was easy we would all have great friends and a great family. Just do what you can do and keep yourself smiling, laughing and in good spirits. Support groups and people should be speaking positive things in your life; they should not be harnessing negative things and/or speaking of negative things.

This is the problem with about 90% of all groups I've seen. This is why my group on Facebook called No More MS Depression is where I teach and preach positive speech, words and thoughts. It is my sincere heart's desire and daily prayer to show everyone that being positive will change the outcome of dealing with the MS. This is also one of the prime reasons I'm writing this book.

Chapter 6

Exercise

In this chapter we will talk about exercise. Exercise has helped me in many ways, not only have I lost 80+ pounds; it has made it easier to get to get up and walk. It will get the blood flowing in places that that did not work as well as they used to like my legs and my hands. Maybe you are affected in your speech, eyes or feet, exercise has a host of health benefits for you. Here are a few:

1. This will contribute to weight Management. This is what most of us want.
2. Exercise combats health conditions like diabetes, heart disease, and blood clots which can lead to many other problems. The improvements to circulation are well studied and well documented.
3. Exercise improves mood. Exercise releases endorphins which help to combat depression. Depression is a major problem not talked about much dealing with MS! Depression issues are usually resolved with a prescription.

4. Exercise will boost your energy. This is another major problem dealing with the MS. The more energy you have the more apt you are to do things. Consequently not only do you have a good attitude and good blood flow, you're starting to lose weight and when you start to feel good your overall outlook is improved. This is one of the pieces of the puzzle to deal with MS. With PMA "positive mental attitude", diet, a good group or groups, this is just a good basis to starting YOUR battle with this monster we call MS. Wake up every day and tell yourself you can do it. Remember your body can do 5%-10% more than that. Never give up. There's someone that is following your lead, you might not know it, you might not see it, but somewhere you are someone's hero. They could be a child, they could be a friend, a husband or wife or close personal family member. These are just a few things that you can do to start your battle and win against MS!

A few tricks I've learned, is to stand when I was in a wheel chair with your back to a corner and put your right foot in front of your left foot. This way the two walls to the side will hold you up. Your brain is learning the muscle memory of balance. Now when this becomes easier, close your eyes, as we try not to let your left shoulder touch the left wall and the right shoulder touch the right wall. Do these for 20 to 30 seconds then switch the position of your feet and put your left foot in front of your right foot.

Another thing to do, when you sit in a chair try making sure the posture of your back is straight, this is very important for your brain to rewire itself to be a better version of what you used to be. The myelin surrounding nerves gets damaged, but can be grown back; the body was made to heal itself. And through a good attitude or PMA, diet, and these exercises amongst others, you can regain everything back, and even be better. I remember at one time I was not able to do five push-ups, now I can do over 25 at 3 to 4 sets. That is 75 to 100 push-ups, coming from a guy who was in a wheelchair, at a hospice less than four years ago. You can do it!

CHAPTER 7

Diet

I n the chapter on diet we will cover the basics to assist you in starting to change your diet so that it becomes a tool in assisting your healing. As you know, this subject is covered in hundreds of books. In order to avoid being overwhelmed by this subject, if you will start making small changes in your diet with basic tools, I believe you'll see big changes in your health. In chapter 10 we mention keeping a log or a journal to chart how you feel after eating certain foods or taking certain medications. This is an excellent tool to help you discover which foods are contributing to your recovery or working against your recovery. In keeping a log, I believe you will discover food sensitivities and or food allergies. Food allergies significantly affect your health. And a person dealing with MS is even more sensitive to the effects of food allergies. This is primarily due to an overworked immune system. Eliminating affecting foods will make significant changes in the way that you feel and the way that you move. Eliminating unhealthy oils and adding healthy oils will significantly improve brain health and brain function. So let's get started.

Fruits and vegetables – the most profound impact one can make in this department is to choose organic. When shopping for fruits and vegetables look for bright colors. Your brightest colored fruits and vegetables contain your highest sources of vitamins, minerals, antioxidants and enzymes. You will receive the greatest concentration of these nutrients by consuming fruits and vegetables at most of your meals. Fruits and vegetables are healthiest when fresh. You have no way of knowing how long ago they were picked. Fresh fruits and vegetables are very expensive, especially when they go bad before you can eat them. I choose to keep a wide variety of fruits and vegetables in my freezer. I happen to live in Wisconsin where the growing season is just a few months long. Having a large supply of fruits and vegetables in my freezer is very handy. If you are having difficulty getting a sufficient amount of healthy vegetables in your diet, try juicing or buy a good blender. Having a smoothie for breakfast will give your system a jolt of live vitamins and minerals in an easily digested form. This one step will get you back into looking forward to having breakfast every day without the tiredness that follows. When preparing vegetables for supper, we will now discuss healthy oils, but first a word on potatoes.

Potatoes – potatoes need special mentioning here. Organic potatoes will cost approximately 2 dollars more for a 5 pound bag. One would think that an organic potato could not be any different from a non-organic potato. You would be very wrong. First let me explain how non-organic potatoes are farmed. Potatoes seeds or tubers are soaked in pesticide before planting. While they are soaking the fields are tilled and sprayed with more pesticide. During the entire growing process the plants are sprayed with more pesticides. After harvesting the potatoes are sprayed again with pesticides and a product to stop root growth. The product they use is called Sprout Stop. This product comes with an extensive list of instructions for first aid if you touch it, inhale it, ingest it, get it in your eyes or get it on your clothes. This is not something I want to put into my body. Haven't you noticed that the potatoes that you buy today don't sprout while they're waiting to be used? You can see that because of the process used in growing potatoes from seed that peeling them prior to cooking won't remove the entire chemical residue. For that reason they are entirely worth every extra penny they cost. This process applies to sweet potatoes also.

Oils – we are all aware that hydrogenated oils are very bad for us. This goes without need for further explanation. Extra virgin olive oil is a basic, affordable oil to use for every day meals. Coconut oil is excellent oil for cooking. It is more expensive, but in my opinion it is worth it. Extra virgin coconut oil adds a flavor and silkiness to whatever you are preparing. Besides hydrogenated oils, stay away from corn oils and vegetable oils. Healthy oils are necessary for repairing myelin. If your diets does not contain sufficient amounts of healthy oils consider supplementing with fish oil capsules.

Fish – in shopping for fish, choose varieties of fish small in size. A small fish has been in the ocean or lake a short amount of time and has the least amount of toxins in its body. Mainly Mercury and PCB's. We know that larger varieties of fish like tuna, mackerel, swordfish and some salmon have high levels of mercury in the meat. Therefore, small varieties will have much smaller toxin levels due to their shorter lives. Varieties of this nature would include sardines, trout, perch and herring. There will be many others. In shopping for shellfish be aware of the origin. Shellfish are filter feeders and they filter water to get the nutrients they need. When they are harvested from highly contaminated waters they become an unsafe food source. Shrimp are filter feeders. Check the container for origin.

Salt – seriously consider purchasing sea salt. Sea salt is unprocessed. There is nothing added to it. It contains trace minerals that are available nowhere else on earth except from the sea. There are dozens of varieties of sea salt to choose from. Sea salt is harvested all over the earth. Each variety has its own trace mineral structure. Personally, I use Himalayan pink salt. After researching sea salts on my own, I chose this one, due to the 84 trace minerals it contains: in alphabetical order, they are actinium, aluminum, antimony, arsenic, astatine, barium, beryllium, bismuth, boron, bromine, cadmium, calcium, carbon, cerium, cesium, chlorine, chromium, cobalt, copper, dysprosium, erbium, europium, fluorine, francium, gadolinium, gallium, germanium, gold, hafnium, holmium, hydrogen, indium, iodine, iridium, iron, lanthanum, lead, lithium, lutetium, magnesium, manganese, mercury, molybdenum, neodymium, neptunium, nickel, niobium, nitrogen, osmium, oxygen, palladium, phosphorus, platinum, plutonium, polonium, potassium, praseodymium, protactinium, radium, rhenium, rhodium, rubidium, ruthenium, samarium, scandium, selenium, silicon, silver, sodium, strontium, sulfur, tantalum, tellurium, terbium, thallium, thorium, thulium, tin, titanium, uranium, vanadium, wolfram, yttrium, ytterbium, zinc and zirconium. I hope that you will research sea salt for yourself, try some and experience its benefits. Common table salt is comprised primarily of sodium and chlorine. Yes, chlorine, the stuff in your pool.

Protein – your daily protein requirements must be met. However you will meet them, with food or with supplements protein nourishes your muscles. Organic free range beef is expensive. There are several ways to consider this option. Organic free range beef is growth hormone free, antibiotic free; grass fed and processed in an anti-cruelty environment. If you decide to try switching to organic free range beef, the beef portion of your meal will be smaller while your vegetable portion will get significantly larger. Your vegetables have a higher nutritional value anyhow. It will be an adjustment for you. In shopping for chicken, look for organic free range, antibiotic free and growth hormone free. Yes, they feed frying chickens growth hormones. After hatching, a baby chick goes to market for processing in 90 days. Adding growth hormones gets that chicken to market in 30 days. There is a huge benefit for the farmer but it is detrimental to our health. Organic chicken is more costly right now, but if enough people demand it from their markets the price will come down. Powdered protein supplements are a complicated subject. The choices in this product are far too numerous to cover. I suggest that you do your homework and Google everything before making a choice. I have a product I use and it is different from the product that Ray uses, we have different needs. Therefore we use different products that accomplish different things while nourishing our muscles. In shopping for a protein supplement, I found Amazon to be very helpful because they list consumer reviews on all their products. This really helped me in making a choice.

Seasonings – seasonings contain a variety of vitamins and minerals also. It would take an entire book to describe the benefits contained in seasonings. Don't let this subject overwhelm you. Everyone has basic seasonings in their kitchens. Try adding a new one once a month. Do a Google search to find the benefits and help you make a choice. In no time your kitchen will be full of great seasonings. During the summer try growing of few plants to provide fresh picked seasonings during the warm months.

Sprouting – sprouting is not a requirement but needs to be discussed. I heard Dr. Oz say that a healthy pinch of sprouts is equal to eating the whole plant. Seeds for sprouting come in single varieties or mixes. Sprouts are a live source of vitamins and minerals in a small package. It is one way to add a higher volume of vegetables to your diet without consuming a large volume of food. Sprouting is very easy. Sprouts require rinsing twice a day. This would be the only area of sprouting that will cause a problem if you miss it. Sprouts get moldy if they're not rinsed.

My thoughts – healthy eating does not take more time but can be a little more expensive. We all vote with our shopping dollars every time we go to our supermarket. Supermarkets stock what sells. If we continue to choose the healthier options at the market and ask for healthier choices the prices will come down as the unhealthy items are no longer in demand. You have the power to make changes.

CHAPTER 8

Looking Forward

In this chapter we will talk about looking forward. I don't look back, ever. Look forward in noticing the small things that we do. Not the big picture. Your focus going forward will be to notice all the little "wins". When you take a half step forward, it's a win. It's better than to not take any steps at all. You want to think about walking and imagine walking. Dream about walking. Remember what it feels like to go on a long walk. This exercise will set up your brain and your cells for walking. Because this is going to keep you forward-looking in what you should be accomplishing. Don't settle for nothing (NO-thing). Always dream and vision something positive, move forward, imagine yourself moving forward, be all that you want to be, do the things you need to do to get to that spot. Don't accept the norm, what MS or what your doctor says MS should be. As a good friend put it, don't be the status quo! You can do more than what you think you can and if you're tired of hurting and you're in pain, remember the body can do 5%-10% more. If you don't believe me watch a show like "Surviving the Cut", or any video for our special forces.

Watch recruits pushed to their limits, and then do 5%-10% MORE! The human body is resilient. This will show you how far they push their bodies therefore you can push your body too. But please know and understand your body is dealing with MS. But please see yourself doing what you want to be doing not what you were doing. Remember you're going forward not backwards. So stop saying what should have been or what I was or what I did in the past and start saying what I'm going to do, what I am and what I'm becoming. This is how I live every day. I tell myself I'm going to do this today and then I will do more tomorrow. See yourself doing this. Motivate yourself to do this. Become what you dream, dream what you will become. The choice is yours!

In other chapters you'll notice that I say to look forward to be forward. The small wins will help you stay motivated to look forward, you will have bad days. Just don't get down, remember you will win. Keep this in mind at all times. None of this will be easy. But, it will be worth it. Like they say, "we can build it again; it will be built a bit better".

Understand to not look what you were, but look to where you want to be. You will be better, keep that in mind, if you keep looking at what you were you never get to where you want to be. Remember I said a half a step, is better than no steps at all, have you tried walking forward while looking backwards? You tend to run into things. That may seem like the problem we face with MS? We are always worried about what we were, and how were going get back to our old self, not knowing we are being built to be a better version of who we were.

CHAPTER 9

Research

In this chapter please look into doing your own research. Find out what works for you. You chose and do not base your choices on what everyone else is doing. Your MS puzzle is unique to you. You will be told many things that could possibly work in your favor, never fail to try something because someone else failed. Just because it did not work for another does not mean it will not work for you. If you try something new and it doesn't work out, stop! Simple.

Those of us on the Internet are in the information age. You can look and find anything you want to find. So when someone tells you they don't know give them a few minutes and let them find it. This goes for you too. I hope that you will learn in this book to go out and get your own information. Find what might work for you, do your research on every drug, every diet, and every exercise that will work for you in your body. As much as I would love to say what you should do will 100% help you, I just cannot promise that. Even though this worked for me and has worked for Jackie Joy, it is no guarantee that is going to work for you. But this does not mean do not try, always try. As part of your research try things like You Tube, Facebook, Twitter or just Google it. There's no reason for you not to have the information. Check anything you find, there are plenty of groups on Facebook, like my group "No More MS Depression" that will give a wealth of knowledge and warnings for links to new research, drugs, diets, or medical fads that are going on in the world today. I really have a problem with people who say bad things about something they have no clue about. Do your own research. It's your body, it's your health. I realize it is tedious, but like I said earlier there are many groups to join that will give you direction towards information that possibly could help you in your fight with the MS or depression or any other negative effect. Do not accept what you do not want. You hear a lot of bad things about CCSVI (chronic cerebral spinal insufficiency) but do your homework. You heard bad things about stem cells, and now they're saying a lot of life saving things about it. It's funny how something is portrayed negative yesterday and great today. This is the reason why you do a lot of research on your own. Nine times out of 10, if there's money involved there will be a positive spin to it and if there's no money, it gets negative press. You need to do your own homework.

CHAPTER 10

How I Feel About Medicine

I could go on all day with this next issue; we are going to talk about medicine. I never say it is not good for you, but why do you need to take medicine just to counteract the other medicine that you are taking?. It truly makes no sense, you take a pill to stop trembling but then it gives you a headache, now you need a pill for the headache. When I say, if they are just told you to eat healthier you will not have these problems. In this book we are doing a chapter (Chapter 7) on diet. It will not be extensive but it is going to be the beginnings of how to start to change your lifestyle. You'll feel better and you'll be better. The best thing of all you won't be on 500 different pills. I was on 27 medications before I left the hospice. Now I take the Copaxone shot and an occasional Benadryl. Like I said there are some medicines you take even though you feel better and you probably do not need to but once again I am not a medical professional! Please consult your doctor's if anything changes that he would need to know that counteracts with the medication. If you do your research like I stated earlier in Chapter 9 you'll notice most of these medicines are made of the same ingredients in the food that you're supposed to eat. Remember educate yourself and be proactive. Do research and try other things, not just one or two things that your doctor may tell you to do, but try more. Keep a log or diary and write down how you feel, make a journal of it. For example, eat broccoli and two hours later write how you feel. Do this for a few weeks and that will tell you how you react to a certain food and/or medicine. This should be done with almost everything you do. Since we deal with something horrible and it took a long time to manifest, do not expect for it to be over in one. two. three or even 4 days. Medicine is a short-term band-aid when you're dealing with a long-term problem. Now I hate to say this, but we all know the money is not in the cure. It's in the prolonging of your sickness that produces revenue. It's funny how we're now at 400,000 people with MS for over 100 years. They don't understand how we get it, don't know how to stop it and can't reverse it. It simply is an outrage. So we must stick together and share information on what we've won and how we dealt with it in the positive. Negativity breeds negativity. Misery loves company; misery also will make you offer pipedreams about cures. When honestly, the cure is you, your attitude and your drive. If this is not true, I want you to tell those soldiers who come home from Iraq missing limbs and are determined to walk and they walk. But the pharmaceutical companies, want you to believe that pills will cure you, although they take away the pain, they even help some body functions; it is by no means a cure. Once again always, ALWAYS take your medicine as prescribed by your doctor.

CHAPTER 11

Quotations

Do not be surprised when a beast acts beastly—Ron Huley

It is not how others treat you that YOU will be judged on. but how YOU react to that treatment!—Ramon H Garcia

Find the funny.—Ramon H Garcia

Worrying is like a rocking chair. Something to do but you go nowhere!—Ramon H Garcia

<paraphrased from movie Van Wilder>

Get busy living, or get busy dying!—RED, Movie Shawshank Redemption

DO not talk negative things into existence.—Ramon H Garcia

DO what YOU can and leave the rest in Faith to GOD! —Ramon H Garcia

Change your outlook; change your outcome.-Ramon H Garcia

Don't be pawn in someone else's chess game of life.-Ramon H Garcia

Be a better version of yourself everyday—Ramon H Garcia

You are worth it—Ramon H Garcia

CHAPTER 12

Challnge Yourself

In this chapter we are going to talk about challenging yourself. We've all heard the doctor say don't overdo it and don't get over heated. This is all very true, but they never tell you what is 'overdoing it'. Well, for me overdoing it means this; say my arms do not seem to want to do what I ask them to do. Let's say I am doing curls and I do five, and I want to do six but I start to strain and struggle. The sweat starts on my forehead, this is a major indicator to me that it is time to stop and rest. Now for some of you it might be sooner or it might be later, the point is to find where your stopping point is and rest. Do not be ashamed of resting for resting is the way your body heals. But remember, you always can do 5%-10% more than your brain tells you. That is why we give up on trying losing weight so quickly. Our brain tells us what we are going to miss out and that is too tough. We should be focusing on what is to be gained not what will be lost. Again, you can do 5%-10% more than what your brain is trying to tell you. Now that doesn't mean to go all out and hurt yourself, be mindful of your body's limits. Know how far you can push your own body but this will take more than just brainpower. It takes muscle memory, blood memory and cell memory. It's a combination of everything, not just the brain. Look at the thought as a warning to what can happen after 5%-10% more of what you can do. I do this all the time if a trainer or therapist tells me to do three more reps, I do five. If someone told me 'no', I showed them 'yes'. This is how I tell MS or any negative effect what I want to do. Do not let MS or that negative effect control what you want. If you take control back from negative things like MS, weight, diabetes, high blood pressure, etc., those things will not lord over you. MS and 100% of all negative things try to take control of you. It is telling you 'no'. Look at this as a challenge. Now if you're anything like me, you win challenges. So if you put MS in that category you will win, like I said when you change your outlook it changes the outcome. Just keep in mind pain is temporary and you are a winner. You face all challenges unfortunately this challenge is not our choice, but it is your choice to win or to lay down and die. I know this hits home and it finds a way into your heart, to stand up and say 'no more', 'I will win, I will beat this'!

CHAPTER 13

The Puzzle

This chapter is written primarily by Jackie Joy. It is my heartfelt desire that you gain an understanding of the concept 'the puzzle'. Throughout this book we mention "a piece of the puzzle", this concept will become a very important tool in your toolbox for dealing with MS. In chapter 1 we discussed your Dr. and getting started. It is important that you have a doctor that you trust and can confide in. A piece of your puzzle might lie in the medication you're taking. In chapter 2 we discussed attitude. We understand that stress causes damage. Therefore, attitude will be one of the pieces in everyone's puzzle. Almost everyone remembers the first MS attack. Most people can relate it to a life changing incident. A stressful event that preceded the attack. In chapter 6 and 7 we discussed diet and exercise. Both of these are also vital pieces in almost everyone's puzzle. In chapter 9, research may or may not hold a piece of your puzzle. There are numerous websites and Facebook pages that track research. Keep yourself educated because exciting things are happening in the area of research, particularly stem cells. Everyone's puzzle has a different number of pieces. Your puzzle may have two or three pieces, while someone else's puzzle may have 10 or 12 pieces. No two MS patients are exactly alike. The medical establishment places labels like relapsing remitting, secondary progressive, progressive relapsing and primary progressive on us. You must ask yourself, how can there be 4 labels to describe so many people where no two are alike. We've mentioned several times to never compare you to another person dealing with MS. Your puzzle is unique. It is as unique as you are. As you discover the pieces to your puzzle, whether they include diet, exercise, stress, allergies, toxins or environmental issues, you will become healthier and stronger. You will experience the effects of dealing with MS fall away.

We need to repeat that it will be of great benefit to you to journal. In keeping a journal of your journey towards wellness, you might discover food sensitivities, chemical sensitivities, issues with certain drugs and the increasing benefits of exercise. Improvement takes time and logging allows you to gauge progress. Progress is always there. Sometimes it's hard to see because it's slow, but it's there. That is why you must never give up. Also, as you discover pieces to your puzzle new pieces will reveal themselves.

As a final comment, researchers tell us they are close to a cure. Honestly, they have been saying this for the last 25 years that I know of. In any case, if they are close you will need a strong healthy body on the day that you take the 'cure'. There is no medicine that reverses a bad diet and muscle atrophy instantly. It is worth the time and the effort to put forth strengthening and nourishing your body. If the cure isn't discovered in your lifetime, most likely you won't need it. You'll already be cured. Understand, there is no revenue in curing anything. I hope you realize that the cure lies within you. It is in your power, it is in your grasp. Go get it.

CHAPTER 14

Final Thoughts

I wasn't quite sure on how to word my final thoughts, for you would not be reading this book if you had not already determined in your heart that you are a winner. I pray that all this starts or stops a final thought in your heart. But since this will not be the last book, there honestly is no such thing as a final thought. Since MS does not stop, your life does not stop therefore there's nothing final. So I'm going to say this; stay the course, never give up, know that everything you do brings you closer to a happy result. Remember this is your race. It's how you run it, knowing you can run this for yourself. Never stop trying to move forward, it is not going to be easy, it is not going to be fun. It will take hard work and discipline. This is why I said in a lot of my chapter's just smile and find the funny in all you do. Only look back to see where you came from to gauge the progress you've made so far. Don't compare a negative with a negative; it will only equal a negative. Stay positive, these are basic instructions on how I dealt with the monster we call MS. You all will face your own form of MS, no matter what a study says, no matter what the numbers say, it is not you.

These are roundabout terms, so in trying to understand how something possibly COULD work, remember no two MS patients are the same and no two people are the same, and so take the information as a guideline in your battle with MS.

These guidelines will give you directions on the street with many turns as you travel toward health. The scientific facts that they find should motivate you to do more research on what they're looking at but always look to see if there is a healthier, natural, alternative to what they're saying. This would be what is best for your body and your mind. Since the mind is 90% involved in MS affliction, always look at things that you put in your body that harm the brain. These things are allies to the demyelization of every nerve cell in your brain, so look to foods that are going to help build up and nourish those nerves; I did the same thing while in hospice. I Googled information that would help rebuild the nerves that were damaged in dealing with MS.

The information is out there and I really wish our medical community would pass more of this info out to patients. Remember, your health is your responsibility; no one can tell you how you feel. I pray this book helps to give you a beginner's guide on how to start to deal with the symptoms and the horrors of MS. But I pray you do it with a smile and know it does not last, your mind makes it worse than it really is. Some doctors and I specify <u>some </u>tell you that there's no hope, THERE IS ALWAYS HOPE! This is why I tell you, never speak negative things into existence. Do not let others make you think negative things into your existence. I pray this all hits home and helps. This is not the end, do not give up, and stay on a positive course.

Thank you, Ramon Hyron Garcia

Dedication

Now this is to acknowledge my son Christian Rey Taijeron Garcia, if it wasn't for him leaving my positive thoughts in this world, I probably would not have made it, I love you son! Even though you're too young to understand what's going on right now, I will always do what I can to make sure I'm strong for you. When you're old enough to read this, I want you to know, throughout most of my pain you are my shining light. You are my blessing from God. No matter what happens in life, I want you to know your Dad loves you. With this I hope all others find their reason to be strong through their negative issues. Son, always be strong for your family. Never give up, there's always sunshine after rain, and sometimes during. Even if it's dark, if you can't find light make your own light. I pray for you every day and every night. You always come first on this earth. Understand at my weakest time the thought of you made me get up and I fell. So too, I pray for you to get up every time you fall, know the difference between falling and someone telling you you fell. Not everyone is looking at your best interests. But you are guaranteed your Dad and God, most of all God will never ever leave you.